9 Steps to Heal Your Resentment and Reboot Your Marriage

9 Steps to Heal Your Resentment and Reboot Your Marriage

Tanja Pajevic

Abbondanza Press
Boulder, CO

Published in the United States by Abbondanza Press
ISBN: 978-0-9863031-1-1

First edition (Version 1.1)

DISCLAIMER

For Ken, Nico, and Gabriel.

CONTENTS

Introduction

A few years ago, I wrote a blog post, "How Resentment Kills a Marriage (and 5 Ways You Can Kill Your Resentment)," that hit a nerve, with hundreds of thousands of readers devouring it in search of help. Since then, I've come to realize that resentment is the #1 issue in our marriages, if not *the* hidden killer. Every day, I get new pleas for help, and that's from folks brave enough to post their comments publicly. Thousands of others visit anonymously, looking for tips.

This whole experience has taught me three things:

1. We're all in the same boat,
2. We need help, and
3. We need it *now!*

Hey, I get it. If I didn't, I never would have written about resentment in the first place. The good news is that this stuff is doable. I've made it to the other side, and so can you.

This book will show you how. That's why I wrote it—because I don't want you to have to suffer through this alone, like I did.

The other reason I wrote this book is to save you time, energy, and money. Because not everyone has five years to spend reading marriage and psychology books in an attempt to save his or her marriage. (Yes, *five*.) Thankfully, all that reading gave me a pretty good idea of what works when it comes to dealing with our resentment. I've boiled down everything I learned into nine easy-to-read steps—a virtual cheat sheet for rebooting your marriage.

If you're wondering whether this stuff works, the answer is *yes*. Everything in this book, I've done myself. And not only have these steps rebooted my marriage, they've rebooted my *life*.

So take heart. You *can* do this. *And you're not alone.*

All you need to do is follow the nine steps. Then do the exercises, because that's where you'll get the most benefit.

But maybe you don't have that much time. Maybe you need help *right now, dammit!* That's why I've broken the nine steps down into smaller tips, to make things even more manageable.

So jump in wherever you want. Try a tip that calls out to you. They try another. But please know that you're going to get the most bang for your buck if you do all nine steps. Doing a few exercises will help, sure, but more in a putting-on-a-Band-Aid kind of way. **If you're looking for serious, long-lasting change, do all nine of the steps.**

Capiche?

And yeah, it might be a little uncomfortable at first. It might be a *lot* uncomfortable. That's OK. Keep going. Your marriage is at stake.

Your life is at stake.

Much love,
Tanja

P.S. Just to be clear, I'm not a therapist. What I am is a mother, wife, sister, friend, writer, reader, impromptu dancer and passionate coffee drinker, as well as a former college instructor and bartender. Meaning that I've spent more than 20 years listening to other people's problems and helping them solve them.

P.P.S. I'm one of those people who actually *likes* boiling down large amounts of information into bite-sized chunks so the rest of us can understand it. Nothing makes me crazier than reading a ridiculously long book that makes no frigging sense because the writer used too many fancy words. So there'll be none of that here.

There will, however, be plenty of joking around, as well as a few swear words—mainly because I have a lot of Balkan blood in me, and that's just part of the package. If you get offended easily, this might not be the book for you. For the rest of you, you're in good hands!

Part 1: What's the Problem, Jack? Identifying and Understanding the Major Players Behind Your Resentment

When I started my *Reboot This Marriage* blog in 2011, I was surprised by how many people came out of the woodwork to tell me about their marital problems. Men and women from all walks of life told me how they wished they'd dealt with their problems earlier—if they had, they might still be married.

The biggest problem, by far, was resentment. I couldn't believe how many people told me that they'd let their resentment fester for years, until it eventually destroyed their marriages.

That doesn't have to be you. So let's get cracking!

Step 1: Figure Out What Makes You Resentful

First, let's figure out what's making you so damn resentful. The more specific we can be, the better. So let's do a simple writing exercise to get started. Grab a pencil or pen and write your answers below. If you prefer, write them in a notebook or journal.

When you're ready, take a few minutes to list everything you're feeling resentful about. If you're like most of us, you'll have a list the size of Antarctica. That's OK! It gives us something to work with.

For those of you who are stuck, here are some of the common problem areas in most marriages:

- **Sex.** Are you having any? Enough?
- **Money.** Who makes it; who spends it. What are the issues here? What do you always fight about?

- **House and home.** Who does what; who's responsible for what. Possible topics include cleaning, mowing, fixing, etc. What do you always argue about?
- **Children.** Who does what; who's responsible for what. Possible topics include child care, parent-teacher communication, sick-child care, sports/activities, play dates, doctor appointments, etc.
- **Parenting.** Are you on the same page? Similar philosophies? Who does what?
- **Meals.** Who cooks, buys groceries, packs lunches, etc.
- **Friends.** Who gets to see their friends; whose friends get left out, etc.
- **In-laws.** Enough said.
- **Hobbies/exercise/alone time.** What?! Alone time? Hobbies? Yes, that's right. Jot them down.
- **Work.** Are you working too much/too little? How about your spouse?
- **Anything else we missed.** Jot it down.

Write your answers below.

Got your list? Good. Now it's time to figure out what to do with it.

Step 2: Learn When to Say Yes and When to Say No

OK, folks, this is where we dig in and figure out what the hell to do with all that information. So let's jump right in with some tips and techniques to help reduce your resentment.

Now that I've got you pissed off and foaming at the mouth, let's start with **three things you no longer want to do and are ready to get off your plate**. List them below or in your journal.

1.

2.

3.

If you've listed more than three things, put an asterisk next to your top three. That's what we're going to tackle first.

TIP #1: RENEGOTIATE.

How can you get these responsibilities off your plate? Can you simply stop doing them? Hire someone to help?

Get creative here, and jot down whatever comes to mind, no matter how crazy it seems. For example, if you're tired of cooking, can you make sandwiches for dinner twice a week? Can you team up with a friend and make monster batches of soups or casseroles to freeze or share? Can you feed your kids cereal for a few days?

Jot down your ideas below.

TIP #2: LOWER YOUR EXPECTATIONS.

I have a friend who regularly eats cereal for dinner. Two friends, actually. And I can't tell you how many women have told me that they don't bother cooking dinner when their husband's out of town.

What?! Who said you have to feed your husband a proper meal every night? He'll survive one or two nights of cold grub, just like the rest of us. Which leads me to:

TIP #3: THE POWER OF NO.

Take a step back and look at your day. If you're like most of us, you have a to-do list that would choke a gorilla. And I'll bet you anything that there are at least one or two things on that list you really, really don't want to do.

So don't do them.

Ack!

I know, this is big. You might have to take a deep breath so you don't go into convulsions. That's OK. Just keep breathing.

If you're like most of us, you're so overscheduled and stressed out that even the *idea* of adding anything else to your plate sends you over the edge.

I get it. That's why **we're going to start by creating some space in your life.** So let's try again.

What one thing can you say no to today?

Write it below.

Now do it!

Every day this week, choose one thing on your list to say no to.

Write those down below.

Monday:
Tuesday:
Wednesday:
Thursday:
Friday:
Saturday:
Sunday:

At the end of your day (or week), jot down what happened when you said no. Write your notes below.

Did the roof fall down? Did your children fall apart because you sent them to school in dirty clothes? Did your spouse freak out because you didn't do the dishes? Did your boss freak out because you didn't answer his late-night email?

Probably not.

Here's what I hope happened instead—that you found a bit more room to breathe. **I hope you found some time for *you.***

Tip #4: The Power of YES.

Now that you've started saying NO to a few things in your life, it's time to figure out what you'd like to say YES to.

That's right! **You get to *choose* something just for you.** (I know, this can be hard to believe in this busy day and age—especially when you're married with young kids.)

So let's figure out what that thing is going to be. What's something that brings you joy? Or something you loved that got pushed out over the years. Go ahead and write that down.

And please, don't edit yourself. Nobody's going to see this stuff unless you show it to them. For now, just keep it to yourself. And remember, it's OK to dream big. (Just like it's OK to dream small.)

Write your notes below.

To help you get started, make a list of at least **20 rewards** or things that make you happy.

1.
2.
3.
4.
5.
6.
7.
8.
9.
10.

11.

12.

13.

14.

15.

16.

17.

18.

19.

20.

If you're stuck, think back to what you liked when you were a kid. Here are some ideas:

- rocking out to your favorite song,
- sitting under a tree,
- watching a movie,
- reading a book,
- meeting a friend for coffee or a drink,
- going for a walk or hike,
- going for a bike ride,
- dancing around your living room,
- going to see live music,
- meeting a friend for a sports date,
- visiting the farmer's market,
- brewing yourself a yummy cup of tea,
- grabbing your favorite microbrew, etc.

If anything on your list feels too big or too indulgent, like watching an entire movie, just do it for a shorter time. For example, read for 15 minutes. Watch half a movie. You get the picture.

Choose one of those rewards and DO IT TODAY.

Experiment with your rewards. Treat yourself to one at the start of your day, in the middle of your day, or after everyone's asleep. Jot down what's most helpful, and cross off what's not.

Bonus: Expand your list to 50 rewards. Keep adding to your list as you discover new things that make you happy.

TIP #5: BEWARE OF SHADOW COMFORTS.

Keep an eye out for rewards or treats that make you feel worse instead of better. Jennifer Louden calls these **shadow comforts**. Here are some examples: eating an entire carton of ice cream when you're upset, shopping when you're feeling anxious, or drinking a six pack of beer after a bad day at work.

It might take a bit of detective work to figure out your shadow comforts, so don't worry about this too much right now. We'll discuss shadow comforts and **numbing** in further detail in a bit. For now, just try to keep an eye out for so-called treats that make you feel yucky.

Step 3: Honor Who You Are and Where You Came From

Now that we have a little forward momentum going, let's explore the deeper roots behind your resentment. I get that your spouse is driving you crazy, *really*—mine still does, and I've been working on this for years. But there's a whole bunch of other stuff going on as well, and now's the time to get to the bottom of it.

COMING TO TERMS WITH OUR PAST AND OUR PRESENT

Did you have a bachelor or bachelorette party before you got married? Most of us, I'm guessing, probably did. It was a way of celebrating our last hurrah as a single person before we moved into our new life.

Now think back to when you became a parent. At that point, the go-to ritual was a baby shower. Sure, it helped us load up on baby gear, and maybe we even got some tips for surviving those early, sleepless months. But did any of that really prepare you for the enormous sea change you were about to undergo? Did any of those baby games prepare you for the fact that your identity was about to drastically change? That life, as you knew it, was basically over?

Probably not.

And this, my friends, is a problem.

TIP #1: STOP LOOKING IN THE REARVIEW MIRROR.

Until we can consciously say good-bye to the people we once were (and the lives we once led), we can't fully move forward. Because some part of us will always be stuck in the past, waiting for something that no longer exists.

This causes so much pain in our lives, not to mention resentment. Because we're no longer the single, independent adults we used to be—and we can't come and go as we please. Now we have a spouse AND a tiny little baby to take care of. And while it's possible to ignore your spouse at times, you can't do that with an infant—not if you want to keep it alive. He or she needs 24/7 care and attention, no matter what.

That can be a hard pill to swallow, and this is often the point in a marriage when we start lashing out at our spouse (if we haven't already). *Holy Jesus, can't he frigging see how hard I'm working and how desperately I need a break?* she thinks. Meanwhile, he's thinking the same thing.

The other thing that's tricky about our new lives is that we're no longer in control. Now we have to ask for *permission* when we want to go out.

And that really sucks.

Now, I'm not trying to say that marriage and parenting are all hard work and no fun—not by any means. There are *so* many gifts that come from being a parent and spouse, and we'll get to them in a minute.

All I'm trying to say is that every time one door opens, another closes. What this means is that if we don't take the time and energy to honor the door that's closing, some part of us will remain stuck in that old life, waiting and wishing for something that no longer exists.

This, my friends, is *big*.

Becoming a spouse and parent is a giant identity shift no matter how you slice it. After all, marriage and parenthood are some of life's biggest transitions. They're also *huge stressors*. And we don't usually comprehend the full scope of this kind of transition while we're going through it.

Until we wake up one day, wondering what happened to our old lives.

How can this not bring up some kind of grief? Even if you're married to the finest person in the world (and have the sweetest, most well-behaved baby), you're going to miss *something* from your old life.

That's what grief is, after all. A sadness or sorrow over something you've lost.

The problem is that our society doesn't recognize that grief. Nor does it teach us that grief is a natural part of the transition process.

But here's what I've learned:

TIP #2: TO HEAL OUR GRIEF, WE MUST ACKNOWLEDGE IT.

In other words, the only way out is through.

When we don't acknowledge grief, we remain stuck. The pressure keeps building and building until, eventually, something gives. This might be you, your sanity, your health, your job, or your marriage.

For some people, this shows up as an outright identity crisis. For others, it manifests as a slow burn. Or maybe it's an uncomfortable feeling you can't quite pin down, a melancholy for what *was*, a low-grade itch you can't quite scratch.

Wherever you are on this spectrum, you probably haven't had the opportunity to slow down and truly honor these momentous changes. So that's what we're going to do today.

It doesn't matter if you've been married for five minutes or 50 years, whether your kids are babies or already in college. Until we get this down on paper, most of us don't realize how strongly our unacknowledged grief has been driving our lives, not to mention fueling our resentments.

My Story

When Ken and I were planning our wedding, I thought I'd dealt with the grief that arose from the loss of my single life. But old habits die hard (especially when you marry later in life), and because the only ceremony I did was a regular ole bachelorette party, I found myself getting pretty squirrelly as the big day approached. So much so that I left the country.

Yikes.

After we got back from our honeymoon, I left again—this time for an entire month.

Double yikes.

Now, both trips were work-related, true. But tell me: who leaves the country for three weeks right before her wedding, then turns around and heads to a month-long writer's retreat (on the opposite coast, no less) right after her honeymoon?

Someone who's afraid of commitment, that's who.

Thankfully, I've gotten a lot better over the years, and thank goodness, my rock-star husband has hung in there with me. He's one of the main reasons I'm the person I am today, and I'm beyond blessed to have him as my partner. But the mere process of being married to the man has broken me down and rebuilt me in ridiculously profound ways. Becoming a mother has done the same. At this point, I'm like the Million Dollar Woman, with few original parts left.

If we do this right, your transformation shouldn't have to be so painful.

So pull out your journal, friend, because it's time to complete the circle. It's time to honor who you are and where you came from.

TIP #3: RECONCILE THE PAST.

Let's start by coming to terms with your past. In this writing exercise, you're going to write about everything you've **lost** through marriage and parenthood. This can include parts of your old life (or old identity) that you miss, such as friends or activities you wish you could carry into your current life.

Set a timer for five minutes. During that time, write whatever comes into your mind, and *don't edit yourself.* This is important. You want to get at the good, juicy stuff beneath the surface, and to get there, we're going to need to bypass the inner-critic-type person who's always on alert. So don't judge whatever comes up. Seriously. Just keep writing.

If you get stuck, just keep moving your hand across the page. If you have to, repeat the same word over and over, until something else comes up. Don't stop until your five minutes are up, and you'll be amazed at what you uncover.

Write your thoughts below or in your journal.

Ready? Go!

TIP #4: RECONCILE THE PRESENT.

Now take five minutes to write about everything you've **gained** through marriage and parenthood. This can include companionship, a warm body to share your bed, someone to do your laundry, a child's sweet hug, you name it.

Same rules as in tip #3. Set your timer for five minutes, start writing, and keep moving your hand across the page. No editing, just keep going.

Write your thoughts below.

Whew! Talk about some intense exercises!

This might be a good place to take a break and think about some of the things that came up during these last two exercises.

Jot down any additional thoughts below.

Bonus: Take a few minutes to share something you gained with your spouse or children. Are you feeling thankful for having them in your life? Tell them.

When you're ready, move on to the following exercise.

TIP #5: CREATE A CEREMONY.

All right, let's wrap this baby up and **create a ceremony** to honor all the kick-ass work you've just done. Choose a ritual that resonates with you, or make up your own. Then do it.

Here are a few ideas to get you started:

RELEASE THE PAST:

- When you're ready to let go of some aspect from your past, rip up your notes from our reconciling-the-past exercise. Throw them away, bury them, or burn them.
- Go outside and pick up a rock that calls to you. Think about the things from your old life that you're ready to release. Imagine you're transferring them into this rock, and then throw it, toss it into a creek, or bury it.
- Burn incense or sage to rid your house of old energy.

- Get rid of (or recycle) any old, unused objects from your old life that no longer fit into your current life or that no longer make you happy.

HONOR THE PRESENT:

- Plant a flower, shrub, or tree to symbolize a new start.
- Create a new family ritual. For example, have everyone share one good and one bad thing from their day at the dinner table, or hold a once-a-week family meeting to check in with each other.
- Start a new family tradition that speaks to you. For example, instead of visiting in-laws each and every holiday, choose one holiday to stay home and create your own family traditions.
- Create a personal (or family) altar. This can be a tiny space nobody knows about except you—a space filled with meaningful objects where you can go to regroup, meditate, or pray.

If you feel like these last few exercises didn't really work for you, try them again. It might take a few more passes at the writing exercises to reach what's buried underneath—especially if your mind is going a mile a minute or if you're stuck in a story of how things *should* be.

Another idea is to write down anything that came up during your ceremony. This can include thoughts, feelings, ideas, or anything you might want to look into further.

Write those below.

TIP #6: TELL THE TRUTH. NOTHING BUT THE TRUTH.

If you're still stuck, **try telling the whole story**. By that, I mean write about the good, the bad, *and* the ugly. Why am I asking you to tell the whole story? Because if you're only telling one half (Everything's awesome! Or: Everything sucks!), chances are you're ignoring a whole other piece of the puzzle. More on this in a bit.

For now, jot down your thoughts below.

These exercises aren't for the faint of heart, folks, and not everybody has the courage to dig in like you just did. So be sure to take a break and honor all your awesome work by doing something fun just for you. Time for one of those rewards!

How First-Family Patterns Affect Our Current Family

Now we're going to go even deeper, and explore some of the patterns we got from our families when we were little.

Tip #7: Deprogram.

The interactions we had with our parents and siblings created background programs that are *still* running in our brains. Much like a computer's operating system, these programs direct the basic ways we think and act, even though we don't often realize it.

Because these programs are always running, they tend to wreak havoc on our lives. *Unless* we're willing to step back and identify them, which is what we're going to do now.

Pull out your pen and paper again, folks. **This is one of the most important exercises in this entire book, so please don't bypass it.**

Set your timer for five minutes. During those five minutes, write about the way your parents interacted, the way you interacted with your siblings, the way everyone interacted with each other, etc.

Again, *don't edit yourself*—just write. Remember: nobody's going to see this except you. So just keep your hand moving across the page and see what comes up.

Here are some ideas to help you get started:

- Your parents' relationship: how things were on the surface/underneath; what they fought about, etc.
- Siblings: how you got along/didn't; who got along with whom, etc.
- Family secrets: what were your family secrets? In your extended family?
- What did you love about your family? What did you dislike?
- How was conflict addressed? Fighting?

Write your thoughts below.

Awesome work, folks! That was a big exercise, and I don't want to underestimate the work you just did. For some of you, these patterns are going to be easy to pinpoint. For others, they're going to be hard as hell.

If these questions bring up a lot of anxiety or if you feel like you can't go there because it's not safe, please get professional support as you work through these issues.

As Anne Lamott so memorably said, "My mind is a bad neighborhood I try not to go into alone." I think that describes most of us at one point or another.

TIP #8: RECOGNIZE OLD PATTERNS.

Now we're going to look at the patterns you've just identified, and see if we can pinpoint how those patterns are playing out in your current family. For example, let's say your mother always criticized you—nothing you ever did was good enough. Come to think of it, your wife does the same, and God, does it suck. Every time she gets on your back, it sends you over the edge.

See the connection?

(Yeah, it *is* pretty frightening.)

So let's see what kinds of connections you can make by yourself. Again, don't edit yourself. Just write down whatever comes up. Five minutes.

Write your notes below.

Here's the key, folks: *when we're feeling triggered by our spouse, it's usually because an old pattern is playing itself out.* That's why it's so important to trace that feeling or pattern back and figure out where it started.

Oftentimes, the person you're really mad at isn't your spouse, but someone from your early life. It's almost always the person who first put that pattern into play.

Once you understand this concept, it's a game changer.

Let me give you another example: let's say your father was a terrible listener. In fact, he outright ignored you most of the time. These days, you find yourself flying off the handle when your spouse doesn't seem to be listening.

What's really going on here? That's right—you're triggered by the ingrained memory of your father not listening, which blows your current issue with your spouse to kingdom come, confusing everything and making it messy as hell.

Do you get it? Are you starting to see the pattern?

(If not, take a break and come back to this exercise after a good night's sleep. Or share your explorations with a loved one or trusted friend who isn't going to use this information against you.)

Once we start to understand this pattern, we can begin to change it.

TIP #9: DON'T PULL THE TRIGGER.

Every time you find yourself feeling overly upset or triggered by the situation at hand, take a step back and ask yourself this simple question:

What's really asking for my attention?

Folks, this is one of the most powerful questions you can ask yourself. It will be a complete game changer, as long as you're willing to play. And you do that by giving yourself the time and space to truly answer this question.

I cannot emphasize how important this is. Go into a closet or bathroom, if you have to. Crawl into bed. Sit outside. Step away from the person or situation that pissed you off and ask yourself what's really asking for attention.

Then *allow* your feelings to come up. Don't try to stifle them, because this will just keep you trapped. Allowing is key. Cry, scream, kick, or do whatever you need to do as those feelings rise to the surface. (This is why you'll want to have some privacy.)

Your feelings will be uncomfortable. If they weren't, you would have moved through them a long time ago. They'll eventually subside, I promise. But first, they'll probably reach an intensity you haven't felt for a while. That's how these things go. Just keep breathing.

For some of you, this process is going to feel way too intense and scary. *If that's the case, please get professional support.*

For everyone else, just keep breathing, and allow your feelings (sadness, anger, rage, etc.) to rise up and move through.

Remember, the only way out is through.

TIP #10: BREAK FREE.

Once you've started to figure out which first-family patterns are wreaking havoc in your life, decide which of those patterns you'd like to change in your current family.

Take a few minutes to write your thoughts below.

What *one* thing can you do today to start to change that pattern?

Write that down below.

Now do it.

Here are some ideas to get you started:

- Take a time-out when you find yourself starting to yell at your husband the same way your mom yelled at your dad.
- Ask yourself what's really going on when you find yourself ignoring your older child the way your mom used to ignore your older brother.
- Talk to your spouse and explain to him/her what you've discovered in these exercises and why you'd like him/her to do X, Y, or Z.

Again, the trick here is to do *what feels right for you.* Identify a place to start, and then just take it one step at a time.

Awesome work, folks! I'm so proud of you for all the deep work you're doing—it's huge, and it's going to pay off handsomely.

The next section is about something we all do, **numbing**, and just like the section on family patterns, it can be a game changer.

HOW AND WHY WE NUMB

So what's numbing?

Numbing is a way of coping without actually dealing with the underlying issue. We numb when we're feeling anxious or uncomfortable and are trying to take the edge off.

TIP #11: FEEL YOUR FEELINGS.

Common ways we numb are:

- drinking,
- overeating,
- working too much,
- shopping,
- mindlessly watching TV,
- constantly checking email/texts/smartphone,
- continuously playing video games,
- overscheduling,
- incessant worrying, and
- gossiping.

What these activities have in common is that they all serve to try and "take the edge off vulnerability, pain and discomfort," writes researcher Brene Brown in her book *The Gifts of Imperfection*. (I highly recommend her TED talks on vulnerability and shame, if you haven't seen them.)

Numbing keeps us detached from what's really going on underneath the surface. While our numbing behaviors often help us feel better for a few moments, once that short-lived high has passed, we often feel even worse. (If this sounds familiar, it is. We called these behaviors **shadow comforts** in Step 2.)

The long-term ramifications are much more profound, as Brown found through her research: **"We cannot selectively numb emotions. When we numb the painful emotions, we also numb the positive emotions."**

Whoa. Think about that one for a minute. What it means is that if you're spending every night drinking in front of the TV, you're probably not feeling good about *anything* in your life. Not your marriage, your job, your kids, or heck, even your friends. In fact, everything in your life probably feels pretty bland and unexciting.

Is that really how you want to live?

Time to pull out your courage, folks, because we're going to take a closer look at how we numb. Remember, we all do it—numbing isn't anything to be ashamed of. But we can't do anything about it until we have some information to work with.

So take out your pen and paper again. Take five minutes to write down some of the ways your numb. (If you're stalled, use the list above for ideas.)

Write your notes below.

The next time you feel the urge to do any of the numbing activities you just identified above, take 10 minutes for yourself and go someplace where you can be alone—outside or in the bedroom, bathroom, or car. Take some deep breaths and let your discomfort rise to the surface.

It's OK to cry. For real.

Keep breathing and let the feelings come. *Remember, if you're able to let them move through you, they'll pass. Fighting your emotions just keeps you stuck.*

Then ask yourself this all-important question: **what's really asking for my attention?**

MY STORY

I've picked hundreds (and quite possibly thousands) of fights with Ken from anxiety or a general discomfort that I couldn't explain. Instead of sitting down and figuring out what was really asking for my attention, I'd start firing off complaints—the house was trashed (again), nobody was picking up after themselves, etc., etc., etc.

But every time I sat down and took a few minutes to figure out what was really bothering me, most of the time it had nothing to do with Ken at all.

Here's an example: while I was writing this book, Gabriel was going through a tough transition to kindergarten. He was having a lot of separation anxiety, which made for some rough times around our house. It took a few weeks for things to settle down, and in those weeks, I'd suddenly started shopping.

Now, I'm not a big shopper—I go out a couple of times a year, buy a few new things, and call it a day. But here I was, suddenly getting a little crazy over finding a sweater. And not just a sweater, but the *perfect* sweater. This, I've come to learn, is one of the ways I numb when I'm stressed out, and it was a clear indicator that there was something going on in my life that I wasn't dealing with.

Ken, meanwhile, started ordering a lot of books. Every time the UPS guy starts frequenting our house with another Amazon package, I know we're in trouble.

And I know that we're *numbing*—in this case, trying to take the edge off our anxiety by buying things.

Once I finally understood what was going on, I sat down with Ken and told him how much Gabriel's separation anxiety had affected me. Turns out Ken was also feeling bad about everything that had been going on, just like me, but *neither one of us had talked about it.*

Duh. Is that crazy or what?

And guess what? Once we figured this out, things settled down pretty quickly. We got Gabriel into a rhythm, helped him with his anxiety over school, and moved on to save the world.

Just kidding! But Ken and I *did* stop fighting, and *that* is always something to be thankful for.

Part 2: Time for Some Fun! How to Heal Your Resentment and Reboot Your Marriage

In the five years I've been writing my blog, one of the most important things I've learned about rebooting my marriage is that I have to reboot myself first.

I know, I know—you were hoping I was going to trash your spouse, right? Yeah, that's where I started, too. I wanted somebody to agree with me when I told them what a jerk Ken could be. (And he can be, on occasion. As can I.)

I learned that nothing changes until I change myself.

I also learned that **it's my responsibility to make myself happy—not my spouse's**.

(I know!)

Once I started taking responsibility for my own life and my own happiness, miracles started to happen.

Sounds hokey, but it's true.

So let's do the same for you.

Step 4: Figure Out What Makes You Happy

Part of what we're going to be doing in this section is teaching you how to reconnect with **your deepest needs and wants**, not who you think you *should* be (or what you should want) now that you're married with children.

As we talked about earlier, we tend to lose some core parts of ourselves once we have children, and the further we drift from who we really are (and what we really want), the more miserable we become. That's why it's so important that we get back on track.

The other reason it's so important is because **90% of our happiness comes from within**.

What?!

According to happiness researcher Shawn Achor, only 10% of our happiness comes from the world around us. That includes your spouse, your children, your job, your friends, your house, etc. It includes everything but you.

Talk about a wake-up call! What this means is that it's time to stop blaming everyone else for our misery. Because we have a hell of a lot more power over our lives than we ever realized. And it's up to us to decide how happy we're going to allow ourselves to be. (For more on this topic, I highly recommend Achor's TED talk, "The Happy Secret to Better Work.")

So let's review a few techniques to help us get our game on.

TIP #1: START YOUR DAY WITH 20 MINUTES OF QUIET TIME EVERY MORNING.

This first technique is designed to help you realign with your true self and help you reconnect with what you want out of your life. I can't even *tell* you how important this is.

And yet, I'll bet 80% of you are going to do your best to ignore this simple little tip. Because we're all so damn busy (not to mention exhausted), and who the hell has time to, *gah!*, wake up early when there are Just. So. Many. Other. Things. To. Do.

Yeah. I get it. I really, really get it.

But here's the thing. When you don't take time to ground yourself in the morning, your kid wakes up grumpy, you accidentally burn your toast, you receive a crappy email from your coworker and the next thing you know, you're cranky as hell AND your day has just swirled out of control.

That's because you're **reacting** to everything that's coming at you. And as we all know, when you've got young kids, there's *always* something coming at you. That's why it's so important to be grounded, so those rapid-fire surprises don't throw you off-kilter. When you take the time and space to reconnect with yourself and what truly matters to you, it's easier to let everything else bounce of your back.

You can do this by sitting in silence before everyone gets up. Or you can journal. You can also imagine how you'd like your day to unfold and play that out in your mind.

For a deeper read on how and why it's so important to take 20 minutes of daily quiet time, I highly recommend Trevor Blake's book, *Three Simple Steps*. This book changed my life, and if you follow his instructions, it'll change yours as well.

TIP #2: OR START YOUR DAY WITH 10 MINUTES OF MEDITATION.

There are different approaches to meditation, but the goal behind all of them is to quiet your mind. Not only does meditation teach us to disconnect from the 50,000 thoughts we have every day (yes, 50,000), but it also helps us reconnect with our truest self.

If that's not enough encouragement for why it would be great to start your day by meditating, you should know that meditation is a proven stress reliever, it strengthens our immune systems, and it increases our mental focus. If we do it regularly, that is.

Pretty cool, right? Here are a few ideas for getting started:

- Jump right in by sitting down and following your breath for 10 minutes. Slowly count to four while you breathe in, then count to four as you breathe out. When thoughts arise (as they will), simply say or think "thinking" and go back to your breath and to your counting. This is a simple meditation technique I learned years ago, and one I still follow.

- A friend of mine (a businesswoman with three young children) swears by the Insight Timer app, which tracks your meditation time on your phone.

- A friend turned me on to David Harshada Wagner on Yogaglo as my mother was dying and it's no exaggeration to say that his meditation videos saved my ass for many months afterwards. He talks you through each meditation and is phenomenal at helping move tough emotions. His videos include meditations to get back to sleep, prepare for a big meeting, or deal with arguments, among many others. (He also has several meditations designed especially for men.)

The other reason I'm harping on meditation is that there's something magical about giving yourself this time and space on a daily basis. Your intuition will become stronger. You'll discover answers to questions that have been bugging you for eons. You'll also tune in—and get completely clear—to what your inner voice is telling you. YOUR inner voice, not what someone else thinks you *should* be doing.

After a while, that voice will start to become your most trusted ally. It'll start showing you the parts of your life that aren't working, as well as the ones that are. It'll start to whisper answers to you when you least expect them, as well as wisdoms you didn't know you needed. And it'll bring you back to *you*—the part of yourself that's been waiting for you to listen for a long, long time.

Essentially, that's what your morning time is—a listening to your soul. And that's gold.

If 10 minutes feels too long, start with five minutes. After a few weeks, add one minute a day until you've worked up to 15-20 minutes a day.

TIP #3: EXERCISE.

I know, I know—I'm getting really obvious here, aren't I? We all know that exercise lowers our stress levels, gets our endorphins going, keeps us healthy, and generally helps us feel better. So why aren't we doing it?

Well, maybe you haven't found the kind of exercise you really love. For years, I struggled through a half-ass jogging routine. Then I joined a gym and spent a year paying my dues on the elliptical. Blech. But it wasn't until I found my current dance class that things finally clicked. Instead of watching the minutes crawl by, I was having a blast. And I was doing it for 60 minutes. While laughing my ass off.

That's the kind of exercise I'm talking about. Something that makes you happy. Something that's *fun*.

So go fishing or meet your buds for a pick-up basketball game, if that's what floats your boat. Go for a walk or a hike or belly dance in public. Seriously, though, find something you *love*. This will make all the difference.

TIP #4: FOLLOW WHAT YOU LOVE.

For this tip, let's resurrect something you loved when you were a kid and bring it back into your current life. This can be any kind of interest or hobby you really loved.

For me, this was dancing. Once I found my current dance class, it changed my life. Not only did it keep me semi-sane during my mother's illness and death, but it's kept me grounded during some of the worst marital and parenting moments of my life.

So what's it going to be? And how can you get started?

Pull out your journal or jot down your ideas below.

Tip #5: Try dancing. Yes, really.

Every day, choose a song and dance your ass off to it. Dance in your living room or in the bathroom, if you have to, but dance like nobody's watching.

Why oh why is she harping on the dancing? you ask.

Because dancing connects the mind and body, and I've found that most of us desperately need that connection. We spend so much of our daily life in our heads, thinking and worrying about everything we have to do and everywhere we have to go, sometimes even forgetting that we actually have a body. But our bodies are where we carry our old emotions.

Dancing releases all that old, stuck energy. That's why you'll want to try this at home, when no one's around. Because you might be surprised at the emotions that pop up once your body starts moving freely.

It might be scary at first. You might not know why you're suddenly crying. That's OK. Just keep breathing and moving. Remember, the key is to release those emotions. We don't want to keep them trapped in our body, because—say it with me—that's what keeps us stuck. Dancing is another way of releasing those emotions so you can heal.

The other super cool thing about dance is that it helped me reclaim my body after two pregnancies and nursing two babies. And that's no small feat.

TIP #6: MAKE IT A HABIT.

Research indicates that it takes **21 days** for a new habit to become ingrained. Once you've figured out which of these techniques you'd like to try, set yourself up for success by doing it 21 days in a row.

Track your progress in your journal or on a calendar. You can also track it below:

☐ Day 1	☐ Day 8	☐ Day 15
☐ Day 2	☐ Day 9	☐ Day 16
☐ Day 3	☐ Day 10	☐ Day 17
☐ Day 4	☐ Day 11	☐ Day 18
☐ Day 5	☐ Day 12	☐ Day 19
☐ Day 6	☐ Day 13	☐ Day 20
☐ Day 7	☐ Day 14	☐ Day 21

TIP #7: LEVERAGE YOUR DOWNTIME.

Let's take a look at how you're spending your free time. Are you using it to take care of yourself, or are you squandering it on TV and other numbing activities?

If you're saying "what free time?" then let's start by adding some into your schedule. Even a short walk or 10-minute break can do wonders for a tired body and soul.

But what I've found is that most people pack their schedules with *shoulds* and *have-tos*. They stay super busy because it eases their anxiety and keeps them from having to deal with some deeper issue. (If you think I'm making this up, go back and re-read the section on **numbing**.)

The problem is that once we have kids, downtime is often the first to go. (This is a crucial part of New Parent Boot Camp, where our children break us down before they rebuild us. But it still sucks.)

The kids continue to grow, and our lives careen forward like an out-of-control train until some kind of crisis derails us. Often, these crises remind us of the importance of taking care of our physical and mental health. So work your physical and mental self-care into your schedule now, before you're forced to.

MY STORY

I had a rough pregnancy with Gabriel. After six weeks of bed rest (and a handful of scary hospitalizations), he was born five weeks early during an emergency C-section.

The weeks leading up to his birth were stressful as hell, which is basically why I spent six straight weeks doing nothing but watching HGTV. (Hint: numbing!) Once he was born and we were both out of the woods, I could finally let my guard down.

Gabriel, not so much. He was an intense little guy who didn't sleep. Meaning that I didn't sleep, either.

This went on for an entire year, culminating with a month-long sleepless stretch around his first birthday.

It wasn't pretty.

I spent a lot of that month sobbing, wondering what was wrong with me and why I was so miserable. (Odd that sleep deprivation and postpartum depression never crossed my mind. Hmm.) Anyway, things finally came to a head while we were visiting my in-laws over the holidays. I was walking by the ocean when I had the most incredible urge to throw myself over a cliff. Literally.

As you might imagine, this scared the shit out of me. So much so that I went looking for a therapist when I got home. I had a 3-year-old and a 1-year-old I wanted to stick around for (not to mention myself), and I needed help. Plus I had a grandfather who'd committed suicide, meaning I wasn't going to mess around with this shit.

Finding a therapist was my first step. This wasn't an overnight process, however. It took months to reignite my inner pilot light and a good year to regain more solid footing in my life.

Along the way, a friend introduced me to my current dance class. This, as I've already said, was a gift from the gods. That was my second step.

My third step was starting to meditate again.

Over the years, I've come to realize that meditating is an important part of **my personal holy trinity:** the non-negotiables that keep me functioning and happy. For me, those non-negotiables are writing, exercising, and meditating. Time and time again, I've learned that I need to do *all three* of these things on a regular basis for me to stay sane and happy.

What are your non-negotiables? What do you need to stay grounded and happy?

Write them below.

Then find a way to work them into your schedule. How can you do that?

Jot down your ideas below.

Now, your non-negotiables are probably totally different from mine. But here's what they should all have in common: they're imperative to your happiness and well-being. **They are how you say YES to yourself.**

This, my friends, is a CRUCIAL step in the rebooting process. Please don't skip it.

Step 5: Reframe and Retrain Your Brain

One of the most important things I've learned while doing this work is just how much power we have when it comes to changing our lives. We can do this by reframing our situation and retraining our brains. Ultimately, the choice is up to us.

So why don't we do it?

Well, maybe you were raised by a family who didn't believe in being happy. Maybe there was a kind of power—even honor—in your house given to suffering. Maybe you were taught that that's what life is—suffering and hard work—and that being unhappy is somehow noble.

Except this is *your* life. Meaning that you get to choose.

So let's turn this equation upside down. We'll start by taking a moment to figure out what kind of **payoff** you're getting from being resentful.

Does it make you feel better? Really? Maybe you have that brief moment where you feel like you've been wronged—*lemme tell you about it!*—and then what? Do you feel better after you've stomped around the house and/or told your friends what a jerk your husband/wife is?

I've found that when I complain about something to others, it takes just enough of the steam out of the equation *so that I don't actually have to do anything to fix it.* But when I don't complain to someone else, the issue continues to eat at me and eventually spurs me to action.

What does staying stuck in that resentment really accomplish, anyway? Besides driving another wedge between you and your honey, that is.

Don't believe me? Think about this Nelson Mandela quote for a while and then tell me what you think: **"Resentment is like drinking poison and then hoping it will kill your enemies."**

Yup.

OK, then. Ready to shake things up? Let's learn how our brain chemistry impacts our resentment. Then I'll show you how to retrain your brain.

TIP #1: REWIRE YOUR BRAIN.

In *Buddha's Brain: The Practical Neuroscience of Happiness, Love, and Wisdom,* Rick Hanson explains how our brains evolved to focus on the bad stuff as way of helping us avoid danger and possible death.

Nowadays, however, we don't face the same challenges we used to, like being eaten by a lion. But our brains are still on high alert, pumping **adrenaline (that fight-or-flight chemical)** throughout our system.

Here's how that plays out today: your boss says something that pisses you off, and the next thing you know, you're ready to rip off his little face. Despite the fact that you're no longer in mortal danger, your brain acts like it is.

Worse yet, the chemical makeup of our brains is designed to make sure we remember the yucky stuff—it's primed to make sure the bad stuff sticks. *"This negativity bias,"* Hanson writes, *"overlooks good news, highlights bad news, and creates anxiety and pessimism."*

But wait! That's not all!

"Your brain is like Velcro for negative experiences and Teflon for positive ones—even though most of your experiences are probably neutral or positive."

Whoa. Read that again: *even though most of our experiences are probably neutral or positive.*

That, my friends, is fucked up.

Because of our brain chemistry, we literally don't remember the good stuff. Unless we choose to consciously focus on it, strengthening the positive neural pathways in our brains.

To do that, try this simple exercise: the next time something good happens, consciously savor it for 20-30 seconds. This imprints the positive memory onto your brain.

Now apply this concept to your spouse. Consciously look for something good, kind, or helpful about him/her, and think about it for 20-30 seconds.

Bonus: Write it down below. By the end of the day, add two more things to your list.

Extra-credit bonus: Thank your spouse for one small, specific thing you're grateful for. Now thank him or her for two or three things. Continue this for a full week. *If you do nothing else, this will shift the entire tenor of your relationship.*

TIP #2: ACCENTUATE THE POSITIVE.

As we learned above, we strengthen our brain's neural pathways with every thought and action. What this means is that we literally create our happiness or our misery with every thought we think. When we choose to focus on hurt, suffering, and anger, we reinforce those negative neural pathways, which then increases our hurt, suffering, and anger.

But when we focus on the positive aspects of our lives (such as a fulfilling friendship), we strengthen our brain's positive neural pathways, which then creates more positive experiences in our lives (such as an increasingly rewarding friendship).

Do you see how this works? It's like a sci-fi film, but more fun, because it's real life. All you have to do is remember that the choice is up to you.

Want a happier life? Spend more time thinking about the positive aspects of your life. Want a crappier life? Keep complaining.

TIP #3: CULTIVATE A GRATITUDE HABIT.

Positive psychology researcher Shawn Achor shares the following tip in the TED talk I mentioned earlier: to retrain your brain, **list three things you're grateful for every day**.

This is how you make **gratitude a habit**. Keep up your list for 21 days in a row, and voila, you've rewired your brain!

Let's start with the first week. (You can continue your list in your journal or on the blank pages at the end of this book.) What are you grateful for?

Write that below.

Day 1:

1.

2.

3.

Day 2:

1.

2.

3.

Day 3:

1.

2.

3.

Day 4:

1.

2.

3.

Day 5:

1.

2.

3.

Day 6:

1.

2.

3.

Day 7:

1.

2.

3.

TIP #4: TELL THE WHOLE STORY.

Over the years, I've noticed that people who stay stuck tend to cling to one part of the story. Maybe they're stuck in the story of what a jerk they married, but they've forgotten how much they once loved that person. Or how kind he/she can be when they really need it.

So let's expand your story to include some positive interactions or good memories about your spouse.

Use the space below to draw a line across the blank page. This represents a simple timeline of your relationship. On the far left, write down the date you met your honey. On the far right, add today's date.

Draw your line below. If you need more space, use your notebook or the empty pages at the end of this book.

Now take 10 minutes to include at least five positive events that transpired during your relationship. Add these to your timeline with an approximate date. Beneath that date, write a few sentences detailing the event.

Examples could include:

- your first date/ how you met,
- something funny your spouse did or said,
- a memorable date or trip,
- the birth of your child,
- watching your spouse connect with your child, etc.

Once you've added five positive events to your timeline, challenge yourself and see if you can come up with five more. These don't have to be big events—they can be as simple as your spouse bringing you a cup of coffee or wrapping you in a hug.

If you need more room to fill out your chart, use the space below or one of the blank pages at the end of the book.

Bonus: Add 10 more positive memories to your timeline.

And remember: the key here is to tell the whole story, not just the bad stuff. Because you really are creating whatever you choose to focus on. So be sure to help those Teflon-coated positive memories stick!

This next tip is more sobering, but important as hell if you have children.

TIP #5: REALIZE THAT CO-PARENTING IS A LIFE SENTENCE.

Understand that you'll remain connected to your spouse through your children forever, even if you get divorced.

I don't think a lot of people understand this concept as they're considering divorce. They seem to think divorce will cut the cord once and for all and make their problems with their spouse simply disappear.

But that's not how it works. You're still going to have to communicate with your ex over anything having to do with the kids, such as visitation schedules, schooling, sports, transportation issues, and holidays. And this will continue for the rest of your life, even when the children are adults. You'll just be covering different territory then, such as grandchildren and holidays.

If you think it's hard to deal with your resentment now, imagine having to live with this resentment *for the rest of your life*. Not only will that suck for you, but it'll be hell for your children.

MY STORY

My parents divorced when I was in junior high school. After four long years in divorce court, they continued to fight bitterly about anything and everything, even after the divorce finally went through. When my brother and I were with my father, he complained bitterly about my mother, and vice versa. This continued into my early 20s, after my father remarried, and until he died.

What my parents didn't realize is that **their resentment kept them connected. It also kept them stuck**. When my father finally did remarry, it was to repeat the same patterns and mistakes he'd made with my mother.

This wreaked havoc on all of our lives. It took me years, not to mention a decent amount of therapy, to break the patterns I'd inherited from my parents.

Don't do that to your kids.

If you can't do this work for yourself, my friend, do it for your children. Don't condemn them to another lifetime of pain and resentment. Break the cycle by showing them a better way.

TIP #6: BE COMPASSIONATE WITH YOURSELF.

There will be times when nothing seems to help, and you're stuck as hell and feeling like crap. When that happens, try the following exercise by psychology professor Kristin Neff, which appears in her book *Self-Compassion: The Proven Power of Being Kind to Yourself*.

Put your hand over your heart and take a deep breath. Repeat the following mantra:

> This is a moment of suffering.
> Suffering is a part of life.
> May I be kind to myself in this moment.
> May I give myself the compassion I need.

Keep your hand on your heart for as long as you want. Feels good, doesn't it?

By accepting your suffering (rather than pushing it away), you acknowledge your pain, which helps ease it. What I find so magical about this exercise is that it essentially teaches you how to be there for yourself.

And that, my friends, is the core of everything we're doing here. We're teaching you how to rely on yourself first and foremost, as well as how to heal yourself instead of waiting for your spouse to do it. This is how you take your power back.

Step 6: Communicate More Clearly and Effectively

There are a few different aspects to learning how to communicate more clearly. First, let's learn how to speak up and ask for help. To do that, we need to figure out what we want. Once we're able to ask for what we want (as well as what we need), we can then move on to improving the way we interact with our spouse.

TIP #1: ASK FOR WHAT YOU NEED.

Let's start by asking for what we **need**. What's something you desperately need help with right now?

Maybe it's asking your spouse to pick up the kids, cook dinner, clean the bathroom, or whatever else it is that you're seething about. Or maybe it's asking for an hour after work to go get some exercise. But this is especially important for men/women who do the lion's share of the work (and I don't just mean at the office).

What one thing can you ask for help with this week? Write it below.

Now do it.

TIP #2: ASK FOR WHAT YOU WANT.

Our wants are the next step up from our most basic needs, and just as important. Some things we want might be to go out with our friends or (gasp) take an afternoon to ourselves. But because these types of wants might not feel absolutely necessary, we shy away from asking.

I understand that. So think of this as an opportunity to build your communication muscles.

Then speak up and ask for exactly what you want. No hemming and hawing here. Just a straight, "I'd like to go meet my friends for a couple of hours tomorrow night. Can you please put the kids to sleep?"

If this feels too challenging, **start small**. Ask your spouse to bring you a fork from the kitchen. Or a cup of coffee.

Once you get the smaller ask down, challenge yourself and ask for something bigger. If you're not sure what to ask for, revisit the reward list we created in Step 2. Choose something from that list and ask for it. Again, ask clearly, without any hemming and hawing.

But what if you're too afraid to ask?

Do you feel like you don't deserve to take some time for yourself? Are you afraid your spouse is going to say no?

Tip #3: Offer to trade.

If that's the case, **offer your spouse something in exchange**. Offer him a night out with his friends while you watch the kids. That way, you both win.

I highly recommend this **win-win scenario** for anyone struggling with this concept, especially if you're feeling guilty for taking time away from the kids. It's a great way to get what you want without being sidelined by guilt.

If you're struggling with your guilt and aren't able to ask for what you want and need because of it, go back and take a look at your family patterns in Step 3.

Who ladled out the guilt when you were a child? Who decided what was good enough, and what wasn't? Your mother? Your father?

Now step back for a moment and look at that person's life. Was she or he happy? Fulfilled?

Probably not. In fact, most people who lay on the guilt do so because they're haunted by their own ghosts. It seems to me, then, that guilting other people becomes an attempt at managing that anxiety. Perhaps it's another way of numbing.

But here's the good news: you don't have to continue this tradition. Part of what it means to become an adult is to cut the cord and differentiate from our parents. This means we become our own person in every sense of the word, from creating our own house rules to stepping into our own beliefs and values.

For many of us, this is lifelong work. That's OK. Just take it one step at a time, my friend, and we'll get there.

Alrighty, then. Back to our regularly scheduled show.

TIP #4: SAY NO TO THE THINGS YOU DON'T WANT TO DO.

Yes, it really is that easy.

(For anyone still wrestling with guilt, saying no to something you don't want to do is going to be a heck of a lot harder. That's why we addressed the larger patterns around family guilt earlier.)

Don't cook tonight if you don't want to—make sandwiches. Don't volunteer for your children's school fundraiser if you don't have the time. *Don't volunteer at all.*

Ack!

Does this induce panic or make you feel anxious? Does it make you think, "I couldn't possibly say no because everyone's doing it," or *"I have to,"* or "what will they think," yadda, yadda, yadda.

If so, I'm going to teach you a life-saving tip:

TIP #5: EVERY TIME YOU SAY YES TO SOMETHING YOU DON'T WANT TO DO, YOU'LL END UP BEING RESENTFUL.

Every time.

Boy, I had to learn this one the hard way. I *continue* to learn this one the hard way.

MY STORY

My younger son loves to fish. If he had his druthers, he'd fish instead of doing anything else, including going to school. Gabriel's the kind of kid who could fish all day. The problem with that is that I'm the kind of mom who can't.

So we try to compromise.

The other day, I let him talk me into staying out way longer than I wanted. I had a yucky feeling in my stomach when I agreed, mainly because I had to rustle up some dinner, and to do that, I still had to hit the grocery store. But we were having such a good time together that I overrode my instincts with rationalizations like "Oh, it'll be fine" and "just this once."

Two hours later, I was tired, hungry, and getting awfully grumpy. And I hate going grocery shopping when I'm hungry.

Gabriel was hungry and grumpy, too, so much so that he had a giant screaming meltdown as we were leaving the lake.

This sucked to high heaven. The only thing worse than your child having a meltdown in public is melting down yourself. Which is what happened next. After doing everything I could think of to get him out of there, I finally snapped and started yelling back.

Talk about feeling like crap! Not only was I pissed about what had just happened, but I was beyond pissed at myself that I'd agreed to stay longer in the first place.

If I'd just followed my instincts and said no in the first place, we could have avoided all that drama. And I could have bypassed all the resentment I felt when things went south. Live and learn, my friends. And learn and learn.

To recap: Say no when you mean no. Seriously.

And careful of those attempts to bypass your intuition, inner wisdom, or gut feelings by telling yourself things like "I don't really want to do this, but I'll do it *just this once*." Beware those Just This Onces. They'll kill you.

For more on this topic, read *The Power of No* by James Altucher and Claudia Altucher.

TIP #6: EVERY TIME YOU SAY YES TO SOMETHING, YOU SAY NO TO SOMETHING ELSE.

For example, let's say you agreed to meet an acquaintance you don't really like. Then one of your favorite people in the world invites you out *on the same day*, but you have to say no, because you've already committed to a person you don't even want to hang out with.

That sucks. And it leads me to this next tip:

TIP #7: DON'T OVERCOMMIT.

When we give away too much of our time and energy, we end up shortchanging our loved ones, not to mention ourselves.

That's what happens to me when I overcommit. By the time I've wrapped up all my obligations, I'm fried and have nothing left for myself, not to mention my family. And because I've pushed myself so far past my limit, we all end up suffering.

So don't overcommit. Because then everything sucks.

All of which leads me to something I recently heard:

TIP #8: IF IT'S NOT A *HELL YES!* IT'S A *NO.*

Wow. Think about that one for a minute. Imagine what your life would look like if you only said yes to the things you *really* wanted to do.

This little technique alone might slice our resentment in half, just like that.

TIP #9: FUCK THE "SHOULDS."

Seriously. Don't ever do anything because you think you should. There's no quicker road to hell than doing something because you think you should.

MY STORY

After a long week of juggling work with wrangling the kids, I'm fried by the time Friday night rolls around. At the end of a busy week, I need downtime to recharge.

Ken's the opposite—he's raring to go.

For a long time, I felt like I *should* be social on Friday nights. But every time we had friends over or went out, it backfired. Because I'd pushed myself beyond my limit, I turned into a grumpy hellion who made life miserable for everyone around me.

Once I realized that I needed to chill out on Fridays, things started falling into place. If we could just regroup and have a movie night instead, then I'd be recharged enough by Saturday to be able to socialize again.

This was a win-win for both of us: Ken got his social time on Saturdays, and I got my downtime on Fridays. And on the plus side, I had way more good (v. evil) energy for my husband and children, which is always good for everyone.

TIP #10: DIVIDE AND CONQUER.

Now that we've talked about some of the bigger issues behind our communication difficulties, let's take a look at some of the common issues driving us all nuts, like **household chores**.

There's just WAY too much work to be done around the house once we have kids. Especially when they're young. It never, *ever* stops. And almost everyone I've spoken with feels resentful about it.

But most of those folks have never taken the time to discuss their expectations around those household chores. So let's do it now.

Set aside 15-20 minutes for you and your honey to sit down together and clarify who's going to do what. Make a list of all the household chores that need to be done on a daily, weekly, monthly, or yearly basis.

Write those below. You can also use a notebook or the space at the end of this book.

Then figure out who likes to do what. For example, if your spouse likes to cook, great. There's no reason you should be struggling in the kitchen when Jimbo enjoys whipping up yummy meals. Sign him up!

Meanwhile, you might hate walking the dog while your wife loves it. Great! Figuring this stuff out is half the battle. Keep going until you've both taken responsibility for chores you don't mind doing.

Write your new chore divisions below.

Then bring your kids into the equation. Even small children can set the table or put away toys. Decide how you'd like to split up these tasks, and add them to the list.

Once you've addressed the easier chores, divvy up the rest. And **compromise**, folks. If you both hate scrubbing toilets, for example, alternate weeks. Exchange one chore for another. But keep talking until you've discussed everything on your list.

Complete your list below, or on a separate piece of paper.

Once you have everything down in black and white, post your list on your fridge, where everyone can see it. If your children are too young to read, add a few simple drawings to represent their chores.

Then stick to them. Consider holding a brief, five-minute check-in every week to chart your progress and keep yourselves accountable.

TIP #11. NEGOTIATE AND RENEGOTIATE.

Remember how we decided that Jimbo was going to cook from now on? Yeah, but we forgot to take into consideration that he doesn't get home until 7:00 p.m. most nights and by that time, the kids have eaten everything in sight and you're all foaming at the mouth.

So let's reconsider. Maybe Jimbo makes a big batch of something on Sunday to get you through the early part of the week. Or you make a slow-cooker recipe mid-week. Maybe you order takeout on Tuesdays.

The trick here is to ASK for what you need. Clearly. Then keep talking and talking and talking until you figure things out.

And this, my friends, is where I see a lot of relationships break down. **It's not enough to telepathically beam your wishes toward your partner.** That might have worked for Mork and Mindy, but it's not going to work for you.

If you're really struggling with asking for what you need, practice with a friend or pick up a book on assertiveness training, but do whatever you need to get those words out of your mouth!

Then repeat as needed. If something's working, great! If not, renegotiate. Nobody said this stuff is set in stone.

If it makes you feel better, Ken and I are STILL renegotiating. And we probably always will be. We make out a new chore chart at few times a year, and we're always refining family rules such as how much TV time the kids can watch.

That's just the nature of living with children. You're always chasing a moving target. That's OK. Keep going.

And keep talking! You're sunk when you stop.

TIP #12: LET GO OF HOW IT'S *SUPPOSED* TO BE DONE. STOP TRYING TO CONTROL EVERYTHING.

Ladies, I'm talking to you on this one. I can't count the number of times I've seen a woman ask her husband for help, then criticize him when he doesn't do it "right."

Talk about creating your own misery!

So stop already. I know—it's hard. We women want things done a certain way, especially when it comes to the kids. I get that.

But who's to say that your way is the right way?

Besides, your husband is a capable adult. If he wasn't, you wouldn't have married him. So trust the guy already. Trust him with the kids, trust him with the chores, and trust him when he does things his way. You're partners, remember?

Because even though you might not like his way of doing things, consider that you might be feeling uncomfortable simply because it's new and different. But kids need that. They need to see that that there's more than one way of doing something. They need to see that the world isn't black and white.

We teach them this by modeling it in our lives and our relationships.

"OK," you say. "But what if I just don't trust my husband with our baby? He's never been alone with her and he doesn't know what to do."

Well, then you have to let him figure it out. How's he going to learn if you're constantly on his back?

He won't.

He'll just stop trying instead, and then you're both back to square one. Except you'll both be a lot more miserable.

So treat your spouse with the respect he deserves. Bite your tongue, if you need to. And remember that you chose this person for a reason.

A word of caution: If you're the kind of wife/husband who insists on always having things your way, letting your spouse do it his/her own way is going to bring up a hell of a lot of anxiety and discomfort.

If that's you, revisit Step 3 to consider whether you're playing out an old family pattern. This will help you clarify how to change this pattern so that you can create a new legacy for your family.

Now on to a different problem.

What if your spouse refuses to help?

TIP #13: WORK THROUGH RESISTANCE.

Oh, boy. This is a serious problem for a lot of folks.

When we start to change things, it can be pretty uncomfortable for the people around us. For many folks, this can be downright threatening. **So they test us to see if we really mean it.** (Just like our kids do when we're trying to implement a new rule.)

If you stick to your guns, they'll come around, eventually. Harriet Lerner explains this process in *The Dance of Anger*, a book I highly recommend if you're trying to make sustainable change with a difficult person in your life.

The trick, of course, is to recognize the pattern once it pops up. When your spouse starts pushing back, it's crucial that you stay the course and stick to the changes you're trying to implement. If you give up and back down, you're back to square one. Recommit to what you're trying to accomplish and things should eventually settle down.

Here's an example from the blog: a reader wrote in to say she'd talked to her spouse and told him she needed one day a week to herself. He said he supported her but did nothing to help her out. She was stuck, pissed at her husband, and about to give up.

So I told her to solve the problem herself—to do a swap with a friend, find a neighbor willing to help out, etc.—by doing whatever she needed to do to get that time for herself. After a while, her husband would realize she was serious and hopefully step up to help.

If he didn't? Well, she could then cross that bridge when she came to it. In the meantime, by taking charge and fixing her own problems, she was taking back her power. This would change everything.

Speaking of taking back your power, this next suggestion is one of my all-time favorites:

TIP #14: STOP DOING HOUSEHOLD CHORES.

In her book *Wishcraft*, Barbara Sher explores how the myth of The Good Woman or The Good Provider keeps us from fulfilling our dreams. "If you don't love doing [housework]," she writes, "*stop*. You're only going to live once."

Make a list of everything you have to do, she says. Then cross out everything you'd stop doing if you were going to die in six months.

> And then stop doing them. Your house may not run right. Your lifestyle may go through some interesting mutations. But no one is going to die, no one will get scurvy, no one's teeth will fall out—and no one is going to throw you out on the street for not being a Good Woman or a Good Provider.

Boy. Think about that one for a minute. Once you bring in the whole mortality piece, it's a game changer. At least it has been for me. There's nothing like losing a loved one to teach you what really matters in life. (Hint: it's not the state of your house.)

But the house still has to be kept up, doesn't it?

Well, maybe and maybe not. In the past few months, I've tried this little experiment myself, and here's what I've found: when I don't put so much time and effort into the house, Ken starts stepping up more. My older son, Nico, has even started helping out a bit with the cooking. Which is beyond awesome.

But the bigger payoff is that I'm not funneling my life force into cleaning instead of into my dreams. My house might be messy, but I'm getting a hell of a lot more done. In fact, I never would have finished this book if I was hell-bent on maintaining a perfect house and cooking from scratch every night.

Which leads me to the following:

Tip #15: Stop waiting to be rescued. Take responsibility for your life and happiness instead.

Too many of us wait for someone or something else to make us happy. We think we'll be happy once we find the perfect spouse, have 2.4 children, get a better job, buy a bigger house, or _____ (fill in the blank). But that puts our power *somewhere out there* instead of keeping it within, where it belongs.

This is one of the KEY ways we get tripped up, by waiting for someone else to fix our lives so we don't have to. We wait for our spouse (or friends, or job) to *make it better* when we're the only ones who can do that. We wait for something—anything—to make us happy.

But it doesn't work. Worse yet, all that waiting and hoping only increases our resentment.

So what do we do about that?

We take back our power. And we do that by taking responsibility for our own lives and our own happiness. Instead of telling others what to do, we tend our own hearth. That's when our resentment starts to disappear.

Everything in this book is meant to help you realize that.

Everything.

TIP #16: STOP PUTTING YOUR ENERGY INTO GUILT AND SELF-SACRIFICE.

Instead, put it into taking awesome care of yourself so you can take awesome care of your loved ones.

There's no better way to take care of your loved ones than by taking care of yourself. Mostly because you can't give what you don't have. What this means is that if you're exhausted, you're not going to have any energy for anyone else. And if you don't treat yourself kindly, you're not going to be treating others kindly, either.

This is why it's so important to be "selfish" enough to take care of yourself. When you sacrifice your lifeblood for someone else, Barbara Sher writes, you "create bonds of guilt."

> If your children look into your eyes and see delight, they've got a good world. If you're so tired and angry you can't enjoy them, what they're going to feel is, "I don't care about my Christmas present or my lunch. Why don't you ever smile?"

Think about that for a second.

Our kids don't want more toys from us, **they want our attention**. They want to be seen and heard. **They want to matter**. And to feel like they matter, **they need connection**.

The same goes for our spouse.

Guilt and self-sacrifice don't foster that connection—they just push us further and further away from each other. And when we've sacrificed our lifeblood to those yucky emotions, we all suffer.

So let's take a minute to identify how we can release our guilt and self-sacrificing ways.

What's a current obligation you can let go of? What's something you do on a daily basis that doesn't really need to be done?

Write your ideas down below.

Now write down one thing you can do just for yourself. This should be a fun, relaxing, rewarding, or rejuvenating activity that you really, really want to do. It should be something that takes awesome, awesome care of *you*.

Write that down here.

Then do it.

If you need a little inspiration, consider the following stories from Sher's *Wishcraft*:

John, 32 years old: "If my mother, instead of making all the beds and making sure I had my lunch, had kept coming in to me—when my bed was unmade and nothing was picked up—and telling me how excited she was about some poem she was writing, I think I'd have had the best life in the world! I think that I'd have felt so enthusiastic about her, so free to go out and do what I wanted, so happy to have some real company instead of a devoted maid who made me feel sad and guilty, that I'd have adapted to the rest."

Grace, 27 years old: "My father was the martyr in my family. There were four of us kids, and he worked for years at a routine job to keep us in braces and vacations. I didn't really know what he believed or felt, except that he thought it was good to be the way he was—self-denying for other people's sake. I could never enjoy the 'selfishness' he made possible for me, because he made me so ashamed of it. There's a happy ending to this story, though. After we all got out of school, my father went through an incredible transformation. He quit his job, pooled his savings with another man, and started a restaurant and jazz club! I swear, I would have worked my way through college if he could only have been himself when I was growing up."

Pretty cool, right? So dump the self-sacrifice once and for all. It'll be better for all of you.

Now that we've plumbed the depths of our communication challenges, let's fine-tune things a bit. Let's start by creating more positive interactions with our spouse.

TIP #17: STAY IN THE BLACK.

In his book *Before Happiness*, Shawn Achor shows us how to turn our lives around by focusing on three positive interactions for each negative one. He calls this the 3:1 ratio, and we're going to use it to reboot your relationship.

Today, I'm going to challenge you to have three positive interactions with your spouse for every yucky one.

Here's how easily you can do this: in the morning, when your spouse wakes up, give her a hug or a kiss. That's one. How about a nice little compliment during breakfast? That's two. Have a good day at work, honey. Three.

You can do this while you're making dinner, or while watching TV. Rub his arm. Hold his hand. Listen to what he's telling you.

This might feel awkward at first, but it'll get easier the more you practice. Before long, it'll be second nature.

TIP #18: LISTEN. JUST LISTEN.

This one's huge. Most of us only listen with one ear when our spouse is talking to us. And this sucks.

So stop multitasking (or, *cough*, checking your phone) when your spouse is trying to tell you something. This simple little trick alone will improve your marriage by leaps and bounds, I promise.

TIP #19: DON'T TRY TO SOLVE HER PROBLEMS.

Men, this one's for you! I've heard so many women complain that their husband never listens. But when he does, he always tries to solve the problem, which just pisses her off more.

Instead, just listen. You can rub her arm or give her a hug if she's having a hard time. Or say something appropriate, like "That sucks." Or: "I'm sorry you're having a hard time." Then shut your mouth. (And if you're a woman who feels the urge to dole out advice, well, listen up, too.)

Fully listening to someone is one of the best gifts we can ever give.

TIP #20: STAY PUT AND STAY OPEN.

Don't walk away or change the subject. And for the love of God, don't give your spouse the silent treatment.

The more you use these types of behaviors, the more distance they create between you and your spouse, until you're more detached than you are connected. Marital researchers John Gottman and David Code consider these types of behaviors silent killers in a marriage. Because once you've **emotionally divorced** yourself from your spouse, there's not a lot left to keep you together.

Let's attack this one by looking at the larger picture first. Then I'll show you how to change the dynamic.

Here's the deal: these kinds of patterns begin in childhood and mirror the kind of attachment we had with our mothers. When any minor mishap occurred, it created a chemical imprint on our brains (called an **amygdala memory**) that sent a rush of **fight-or-flight**

hormones coursing through our system. (Remember those fight-or-flight chemicals we talked about in Step 5?)

As we mentioned earlier, the purpose of those fight-or-flight chemicals is to keep us safe. According to David Code in his book *To Raise Happy Kids, Put Your Marriage First*, they also work to keep us from having to experience the same pain twice.

> Unfortunately, the amygdala never forgets an insult, so we carry these anxious, hypervigilant, overreactive memories into our adult relationships. We then overreact to something our loved one says, and we can't explain why. We simply can't remember the original incident with Mommy that caused the amygdala to lay down its once-bitten, twice-shy warning in the first place, years ago.

Yikes!

Here's how this plays out in our current relationships:

> In a sense, many spouses are stuck in fight-or-flight mode and unconsciously seek someone to fight with (or flee from). Blaming Our Spouse is a vicious circle that can become a downward spiral that sours our marriages. It starts with anxious irritability that makes us trigger-happy with our fight response. Next, we either provoke, or feel provoked by, our spouse, so we unleash what we perceive to be a counterattack. This either simmers as tension be-

tween the couple, or escalates into open conflict. Either way, it creates an amygdala memory that leaves both spouses even more reactive to each other the next time around.

This is why it's so frigging important we learn to break these patterns. **The more you run away (or distance yourself) from your spouse, the more fight-or-flight imprints you create on your brain, and the worse your problems become.**

So the next time you're tempted to run away (or give your spouse the silent treatment), take a step back and check your anxiety. **Figure out what's really asking for your attention.** (Remember this tip from Step 3? It's seriously important.)

When you feel your temper rising, tell your spouse you need a time-out and will be back. Then give yourself some time and space to figure out what's really asking for your attention.

Perhaps you're upset about something from work, or worried about an overdue bill. Maybe you even have some low-level anxiety over your child's report card.

Keep digging until you figure it out. Once the light bulb goes on, you'll probably feel a hell of a lot calmer. Once you feel better, you can then reconnect with your spouse.

Don't forget to reconnect.

Every time you reconnect with your loved one, you're reinforcing the positive neural pathways in your brain (instead of the negative ones you were reinforcing when you ran away). These continue to build over time, lowering the stress (and fight-or-flight hormones) you felt when you were fighting with your honey.

So keep at this one, folks! It's a serious game-changer.

TIP #21: REMEMBER, THEY LEARN IT FROM YOU.

Believe it or not, this same pattern plays out with your children.

According to Code, your kids' behavior is a clear indicator of the level of tension in your own life. Meaning if you're having marital problems, your child (who's attuned to you in the same way you were attuned to your parents) has picked up on that anxiety. This sets off her own amygdala warning bells (as well as her fight-or-flight hormones), and before you know it, she's acting out in some way, perhaps by falling in with a bad crowd or having problems at school.

Meanwhile, the real problem is the underlying anxiety she's picking up from you.

So the next time your child starts freaking out, take a look at what's going on in your life or your marriage and pinpoint the source of that tension. Chances are that's the real source of your child's problem.

Whew! You guys rock. If you haven't taken a break already, treat yourself to another reward before we kick into the next section. Because the next couple of steps are going to take things to a whole new level. And they're fun!

Step 7: Learn to Have Fun Again

I've found that one of the hardest things about marriage and parenthood is all that added responsibility. We miss the freedom and excitement of our old lives—at least I do! Sometimes it feels like there's nothing but work, work, and more work staring me in the face.

So let's do what we can to bring back in some fun and excitement. God knows we need it!

TIP #1: HAVE REGULAR DATE NIGHTS.

Yeah, yeah. We all know we're supposed to be doing this one. But it's expensive and we've got to get a sitter and then half the time we end up fighting! It's no wonder our date night falls off the face of the planet as soon as we hit a few snags in the road.

So shake things up a bit. Meet for lunch or a happy hour instead. Go for a hike or a bike ride. See a concert instead of going out to dinner and a movie. The sky's the limit here, folks. Do what feels right for you.

TIP #2: TRY A POOR MAN'S DATE.

After a few expensive, not-so-great date nights, Ken and I started joking about ways to get a few minutes together without having to break the bank.

Below are a few suggestions to help you come up with your own ideas. Hint: don't let the word "date" trip you up.

- Ask relatives/friends to watch the kids for a couple of hours.
- Swap child care with friends, or join a babysitting co-op.
- Sit next to your spouse at dinner (instead of across from him/her). Research shows that men prefer to communicate in a side-by-side fashion rather than facing each other, as women do.
- Let the kids read or draw during dinner so you can actually have a conversation with your sweetie.
- Let your kids eat dinner in front of a video while you and your honey sit at the (gasp) dinner table alone (gasp!).
- Put the kids in front of a video and fool around. Really.
- Hug/sit close for five minutes as a quick reset.

Get creative here. Think outside the box. None of these ideas are groundbreaking, but when Ken and I are stretched to the max, with no dates in sight, they help us reconnect with each other.

And connecting for even a few minutes can be a life-saver.

Tip #3: Revisit your old haunts.

What kinds of activities did you enjoy together before having kids? Did you love to see live music? Then find a way to do that. For example, find a free, local concert, or hit a child-friendly, all-day music festival.

Take a minute to jot down a few activities you and your honey-bunny liked to do before your kiddos came along.

Write those below.

Choose one activity and work it into your schedule in the next week.

TIP #4: FIND SOMEONE ELSE TO JOIN YOU FOR YOUR FAVORITE HOBBY.

Instead of pressuring your spouse to spend his precious free time doing what *you* love, set him free and invite a friend instead. Find someone who loves that hobby as much as you do.

This can be such a gift to the spouse who's always expected to come along. I promise, you'll both have a much better time.

TIP #5: EVERY SO OFTEN, DO SOMETHING YOUR SPOUSE LOVES (EVEN IF YOU DON'T).

Again, this can be such a gift to your spouse, especially if she's used to always hitting the movies alone.

The trick is to join her on these outings only when you can do so with a clear and generous heart. If you're feeling resentful, do yourselves both a favor and pass.

TIP #6: STOP EXPECTING YOUR SPOUSE TO BE YOUR BE-ALL, END-ALL.

He might be your best friend, and if that's the case, you're lucky. But even if he is your best friend, you'll still need other friends. Expecting your spouse to fulfill your every last need sets you both up for failure.

Because it's not realistic. Never mind what the movies have taught you. Those are made-up stories, folks. That happily-ever-after stuff is a *frozen picture in time,* not real life. Real life is a moving target. (More on this in a bit.)

TIP #7: DO SOMETHING FUN AS A FAMILY.

Instead of spending all of your weekend time catching up on household chores, make sure you do something fun together as a family. I often see families split up over the weekend, with the mother taking one kid while the father takes the other. That's fine. But make sure to include some good quality family time in the mix.

Take a few minutes to jot down some ideas for this upcoming weekend. Stretch yourself. Include some of your favorite activities as well as your spouse's. What have the kids been bugging you to do forever?

Mix it up. Then jot down your ideas below.

TIP #8: SEX. HAVE SOME.

I can't count the number of people who've told me they stopped having sex after their second or third kid. Yikes!

Things get crazy once you have a baby, I get that. Plus, you're exhausted as hell. Fair enough. That's why all these other parts of the puzzle are so important—having time to yourself, learning how to ask for what you want, etc. Once you take care of the larger communication issues, you should have a bit more energy for some good, old-fashioned messing around. I hope!

Ladies, here's why this is a big deal: for a lot of guys, sex is how they get close. It's how they communicate. Meaning that coming on to you might be one of the only ways your guy allows himself to be vulnerable, and that takes a lot of courage. So it sucks to high heaven to be shut down.

So start talking, folks. (And yes, I'm talking to both of you.)

Find a way to connect.

But don't, for the love of God, withhold sex as a punishment. (If that's your issue, go back to Step 2 and start over. Do not pass Go.)

TACTICAL TIPS:

- **Just do it.** The longer you go without having sex, the harder it is to get back in the saddle. And I'm sorry to say that I know too many couples who didn't have sex for a full year after having a child.

- **Not interested?** Don't knock it until you try it. I recently watched a TED talk called "The Sex-Starved Marriage" by Michele Weiner-Davis on this topic. In the video, she talks about how women in particular might not feel the urge until they actually start fooling around a bit. Experiment with this. See what works for you.

- **No time? Make time.** Meet up after the kids are asleep, put them in front of a video, send them to a neighbor's, etc.

- **Experiment with time and place.** What time of day do you like to fool around? Where? How about your spouse? Experiment. Shake things up a bit. See what happens.

- **He likes this and I like that.** Yeah, well, this is where all that good communication work we just did comes into play. The more you can communicate *outside* the bedroom, the better your communication *inside* the bedroom.

- **Respect each other's boundaries.** 'Nuff said.

Step 8: Decide What Kind of Marriage You Want to Have

Yup, that's right—you get to choose!

So many of us were socialized to believe that our lives were supposed to look a certain way. First, we had to get a job, then find the perfect spouse, get married, buy a house, have 2.4 kids, then work our asses off until retirement. Yuck!

None of that takes into consideration what YOU want from your life.

And who the hell wants to wait until they're nearly dead before they get to really live their lives? I don't.

So let's take a look at what we want for our lives now. And let's take a look at what we want for our marriages *now*, before it's too late.

TIP #1: LET GO OF THE FAIRY TALE. BECOME YOUR OWN KNIGHT IN SHINING ARMOR.

If you take away nothing else from this book, remember this: **we all need to take responsibility for our own happiness.**

Mainstream media have done marriage a giant disservice by training us to expect a fairy-tale ending that's completely unrealistic. Because of this, most of us are working our asses off, trying to pretend our lives are just as awesome as they are on TV (not to mention as awesome as our friends' lives appear on Facebook).

But we're growing, living, breathing things who aren't designed to stay shiny and new forever. We're human, after all. And we're imperfect.

Therein lies the tension. Beneath our frantic attempts to keep everything perfect-looking lies real life. And real life is messy. Meaning the dam's about to break, with new cracks springing up every day.

Don't be one of those couples who end up divorced because they couldn't understand how to fit into the fairy-tale mold. Nobody can. Instead, **create your own mold.**

TIP #2: IDENTIFY YOUR OWN ROLE MODELS.

Look around you. How many realistic role models for a happy marriage do you see around you?

Very few, probably.

Even friends we consider happily married probably aren't sharing their dirty laundry with us—at least not until they've had a couple of cocktails. *Then* you might hear how their spouse is driving them nuts. Until then, we often assume that everyone's doing it better than we are. That's bullshit.

If someone tells you they have a perfect marriage, don't believe them. Nobody does. *Nobody.*

If you're still not convinced, look back at all the couples you knew 10 years ago. Notice how many "perfect" couples have since split or divorced.

The people you want to look to as role models are those who've been through some serious shit and survived. People like your grandparents, or the couple down the road who raised young children while taking care of aging parents.

Or maybe it's the couple who argues in public (gasp) before actually solving their problems. Or the husband who goes grocery shopping alongside his wife. Maybe it's the woman who started her own part-time business so she could spend more time with her family. Or the guy who spends weekends with his family instead of hanging out at the bars with his buddies. Whatever. These people can be any race, color, creed, or sexual orientation—but something about their lives speaks to you.

Identify those people. Notice what they're doing that's different, and then think of ways you can incorporate that into your own life.

Then write it all down in your journal. Or use the space below.

Bonus exercise: Invite one of your role models out for coffee, a drink, or over for dinner. Get to know them. Ask questions. And listen when they answer.

It's been said that we're the sum of the five people we spend the most time with. Really think about that. If all your friends do is complain about their spouses, then it might be time to widen your social circle.

TIP #3: BUILD A MARRIAGE THAT WORKS FOR YOU AND YOUR SPOUSE, NOT FOR ANYONE ELSE.

Spoiler alert: it's no longer 1950, so you don't have to follow anyone else's crazy rules. You don't have to have a marriage that looks like your parents', or one that looks like your neighbors'. **What you need to have is a marriage that looks like you.**

I can't stress this enough. Your marriage should be unique to you.

So sit down with your spouse and discuss what your ideal marriage would look like for both of you. Really get in there and discuss gender roles, as well as question assumptions. Allow yourselves to consider alternative options.

Take a few minutes to jot down your initial ideas below.

TIP #4: RECONSIDER THE PURPOSE OF MARRIAGE.

In his book *Marriage Rebranded,* author Tyler Ward suggests we reconsider the purpose of marriage. What if the role of marriage isn't just to fall in love? he asks. What if the real role of marriage is to challenge us and help us grow?

Think about that one. It's a biggie.

A lot of us think we're "safe" once we're married. We've got the job, house, partner, and kids—a home run. That's the American Dream, after all. Now we get to kick back and enjoy the scenery.

But that's not how marriage works.

Because marriage isn't stagnant—it's a living, breathing thing. That means it's always changing. And the people who thrive in their marriages are the ones who understand this, and adapt.

The people who don't adapt get stuck. Or worse yet, divorced.

A healthy marriage is a place of growth. It's a safe haven where we challenge each other to become better versions of ourselves. We do this by holding up a light at certain times; at other times, a mirror.

At its core, marriage illuminates the areas where we need to grow.

And that, my friends, is a gift. It might not feel like it when you're in the midst of a challenging time, sure. But once you're further down the road and that particular challenge is nothing more than a distant memory, you'll understand this for the giant gift it is. Because we can do almost anything when someone's got our back.

TIP #5: DECIDE YOU'RE GOING TO STAY MARRIED, NO MATTER WHAT.

Most of us, I've found, are constantly debating whether or not we're safe in our marriages (not to mention the rest of our lives). We're constantly scanning the horizon for signs of trouble, and when that trouble hits, we're outta here. Our fight-or-flight instinct has kicked in, and our stress levels are through the roof.

Remember Step 5 and that whole idea of reprogramming our brains? All that stuff about neural pathways, and how we get to choose whether we're going to strengthen our positive neural pathways or our negative ones?

Well, deciding to stay married is going to help you strengthen those particular neural pathways. Because if you've always got one foot out the door, you're in trouble. You'll see more trouble in your marriage, you'll remember more trouble, and pretty soon, your neural pathways will *create* more trouble.

But when you (and your spouse) decide you're going to stay married *no matter what*, the entire terrain changes. Now you're in for an adventure.

Instead of seeing a fight as a one-way ticket to divorce, it becomes an *opportunity* for you and your spouse to learn to communicate more clearly. **It becomes an opportunity for you to become closer.**

Fully committing to your spouse can be one of the biggest gifts you can ever give someone. I mean, when's the last time you felt that someone was there for you *no matter what*?

Maybe you felt it with your best friend. Or a parent, grandparent, or sibling. So why don't we feel that way with our spouses?

Because we're afraid. We're afraid they're going to leave us or break our hearts. Once you take that possibility out of the equation, everything becomes so much more manageable. Our anxiety levels drop, and life starts to kick ass.

TIP #6: TEND YOUR GARDEN.

Some people believe that marriage requires a lot of work. Others compare it to a garden, a living, growing thing.

I like this metaphor because a) it's positive and b) it's true. To have a successful garden, you need to take good care of it. Plant what you want to grow, then tend it. Water regularly, and weed out the yucky stuff.

Do this with your marriage, and everything will fall into place. Water your spouse with compliments, hugs, kisses, and love. And be sure to take care of the weeds— especially anger and resentment. Ignore them, and they'll choke the life out of your marriage.

TIP #7: STOP CARING ABOUT WHAT OTHERS THINK.

Let go of what others think about your marriage. Stop caring about what others think about your parenting or about the state of your house. *Let go of it all.*

The quickest road to a miserable life is trying to bend yourself into someone you think you're *supposed* to be. Let go of all of that crap, and step into the joy that comes from being the person you really are.

Step 9: Decide What Kind of Life You Want to Have

There's one last, important step to healing your resentment and it's this: remember that this is YOUR life. Yours—not anyone else's.

I say this NOT to encourage you to leave your marriage, but to encourage you to fully live your life.

The truth is, your marriage is only one part of your life, and it might not be the problem. Your failure to follow your dreams might be the problem. Constantly compromising your life might be the problem. *Playing small might be the problem.*

Remember: what you put your energy into expands. Meaning that when I spend all my time complaining about my marriage, you can bet that Ken and I are in for some shitty days.

But when I focus on the things that make me happy, the whole equation changes. Same for when I focus on being thankful for my amazing husband instead of looking for his flaws.

TIP #1: BE GRATEFUL.

Start your day by being grateful, and that gratitude will infuse your entire day. I learned the following exercise from David Harshada Wagner and it's a fun one.

Start by closing your eyes and taking a few minutes to envision all the people you're grateful for. Imagine them surrounding you.

Then take another few minutes to be thankful for the physical things in your life that you're grateful for, such as a roof over your head, the chair you're sitting on, etc.

Finally, take another few minutes to be thankful for all of the gifts your body provides. (If you have health issues, be thankful for aspects you might otherwise take for granted, such as your eyesight or hearing.)

What are we doing here? That's right—we're strengthening our positive neural pathways!

Carry this energy of gratitude into your day.

TIP #2: FOLLOW YOUR DREAMS. START SMALL, BUT *START*.

If you still don't know what you want to do with your life, revisit the reward list we made way back in Step 2. Whatever made you so damn happy when you were little is probably still going to make you pretty damn happy today. Work this into your schedule.

How will you do this?

Start by jotting down some ideas below.

If you're chasing a bigger dream, break it down into manageable tasks. Let's say you've always dreamed about becoming a teacher but work in a different industry. Let's break down the steps you'd need to take to become a teacher:

- Email your local university to have them send you an informational packet on their teacher training certification program.
- Talk with a local teacher to learn what teaching is like on a day-to-day basis.
- Contact your local school to set up a classroom observation.
- Contact your local school to volunteer (and make sure you like teaching).
- Break down the school application process into smaller steps: recommendation letters, tests you'll need to take, additional paperwork, etc.
- Keep going until you've reached your goal.

Now it's your turn. Write down three small baby steps to get you closer to your dream.

1.

2.

3.

Next, schedule them in your planner.
Then *do them*.

TIP #3: BE AUTHENTIC.

There's only one of you in this world, and she/he is *magnificent*.

Hell, yeah, I mean that! Why are you using your incredibly awesome self (with all its incredibly awesome power) to punish yourself? Use it to uplift yourself instead.

Everyone in your life will benefit. Because when you let your light shine, you encourage others to do the same. As Marianne Williamson says in her book, *A Return to Love*:

> We ask ourselves, Who am I to be brilliant, gorgeous, talented, fabulous? Actually, who are you not to be? You are a child of God. Your playing small does not serve the world. There is nothing enlightened about shrinking so that other people won't feel insecure around you. We are all meant to shine, as children do. And as we let our own light shine, we unconsciously give other people permission to do the same.

TIP #4: DECIDE WHETHER YOU'RE GOING TO BE A VICTIM IN YOUR LIFE OR THE CREATOR.

Albert Einstein thought that one of the most important questions we face in this lifetime is deciding whether or not the universe is a friendly place. Does it work for us, or against us?

In other words, are we going to be victims of circumstance, or are we going to be creators?

You know where I stand on this one!

TIP #5: LEARN HOW TO MANAGE YOUR ENERGY. AND STOP WHEN YOU STILL HAVE 10% LEFT.

This life-saving little tip comes from life coach Jennifer Louden, and it's a game-changer. Instead of pushing yourself past the point of exhaustion, stop when you still have a little gas left in the tank. Because when you push yourself past the point of exhaustion, you're going to suffer. Your work will suffer, your life will suffer, and your loved ones will suffer. Remember: you can't give what you don't have.

So stop when you still have 10% left in your tank.

All right, folks, we're nearing the end. But I have to give you one very last tip because it's just so damn important.

TIP # 6: LET IT GO. LIFE IS SHORT.

The single, most important reason for letting go of your resentment and getting your life back on track is because **we're all going to die**. Do you really want to waste the time you have left by being resentful?

In her book *The Top Five Regrets of the Dying*, nurse Bronnie Ware shares the most common regrets of the dying. Here they are:

1. I wish I'd had the courage to live a life true to myself, not the life others expected of me.
2. I wish I hadn't worked so hard.
3. I wish I'd had the courage to express my feelings.
4. I wish I'd stayed in touch with my friends.
5. I wish I'd let myself be happier.

Think about those for a while.

Many of Ware's patients didn't realize they had a choice about this stuff until they were on their deathbed. But you're luckier than that—you're realizing it *now*.

And that's a giant gift.

So don't wait until you're faced with a life-threatening illness or the loss of a loved one before deciding to fully live your life.

That's what happened to me. My mother's death became the catalyst I needed to make these changes truly stick. It was a brutal lesson, and I wish I'd found a way to live more fully earlier. That's OK. I'm learning now, and you can, too.

So make your life matter now, my friend. Because the present is all we have.

So say what you think. Hug your loved ones. Live the life that's right for you, and above all, allow yourself to be happy.

You deserve it.

Thank You

Thank you for taking a chance on this book and the *9 Step* process.

It would mean the world to me if you'd give this book an honest, heartfelt review on the website where you purchased this book. The more reviews this book has, the better its chances of reaching and helping more people. My sincere thanks in advance!

If you feel moved to mention this book on Facebook, Twitter, or any of your other social media feeds, that would also be super-awesome (as would spreading the word in, *gasp*, person). Thank you.

Now it's my turn. I'd like to give you two free gifts just for buying this book.

The first is my report, **"13 Ways to Reboot Your Marriage."** You can claim that by visiting http://RebootThisMarriage.com or by accessing this link: http://bit.ly/1HuSKUD.

My second gift is the report, **"25 Ways to Navigate Your Grief."** You can claim that by visiting http://www.TheRhythmofGrief.com or by accessing this link: http://bit.ly/1BcsCX5.

Again, from the bottom of my heart, thank you.

Much love,
Tanja

P.S. Stay in touch and let me know how it goes. Visit us at http://RebootThisMarriage.com. I can't wait to hear from you!

References

Achor, Shawn. *Before Happiness: The 5 Hidden Keys to Achieving Success, Spreading Happiness, and Sustaining Positive Change.* New York: Crown Business, 2013.

Altucher, James and Claudia Azula Altucher. *The Power of No: Because One Little Word Can Bring Health, Abundance, and Happiness.* Carlsbad, CA: Hay House, Inc., 2014.

Blake, Trevor G. *Three Simple Steps: A Map to Success in Business and Life.* Dallas, TX: BenBella Books, 2012.

Brown, Brene. *The Gifts of Imperfection: Let Go of Who You Think You're Supposed to Be and Embrace Who You Are.* Center City, MN: Hazelden, 2010.

Code, David. *To Raise Happy Kids, Put Your Marriage First.* The Crossroad Publishing Company, 2009.

Hanson, Rick, Ph.D., and Richard Mendius, M.D. *Buddha's Brain: The Practical Neuroscience of Happiness, Love, and Wisdom.* Oakland, CA: New Harbinger Publications, 2009.

Lerner, Harriet, Ph.D. *The Dance of Anger: A Woman's Guide to Changing the Patterns of Intimate Relationships.* William Morrow Paperbacks, 2014.

Neff, Kristin, Ph.D. *Self-Compassion: The Proven Power of Being Kind to Yourself.* New York: Harper Collins, 2011.

Sher, Barbara and Annie Gottlieb. *Wishcraft: How to Get What You Really Want.* New York: Ballantine Books, 2004.

Ward, Tyler. *Marriage Rebranded: Modern Misconceptions & the Unnatural Art of Loving Another Person.* Chicago, IL: Moody Publishers, 2014.

Ware, Bronnie. *The Top Five Regrets of the Dying: A Life Transformed by the Dearly Departed.* Carlsbad CA: Hay House, Inc., 2012.

Acknowledgments

First and foremost, thank you. This book wouldn't exist without the thousands of readers who told me they needed help with their resentment. Thanks to everyone who shared their marital and parenting frustrations with me on the blog, via email, or in real life. This book is for you. I hope it provides you with a roadmap through the quicksand.

Thanks also to the friends who candidly shared their new marriage and mothering challenges back in the day, encouraging me to voice my own.

Giant thanks to everyone who encouraged me in my early blogging days, when I was still writing about playing chicken with the laundry and hadn't yet delved into the more serious stuff.

Heartfelt (and highly caffeinated) thanks to my brother, Dean Pajevic, kind soul and webmaster extraordinaire, for his talented blog and tech support.

Sincere thanks to Thomas McGee for his beautiful cover design.

Deep thanks to Hynek Palatin for his patience, support, and technical wizardry in interior design.

Heartfelt thanks to Rachel Manzo for her kick-ass editorial clarity, and Susanna Donato for her kind, thoughtful, and supportive editing.

There are so many teachers, mentors, and friends whose support throughout the years was instrumental in creating this book; to name them all would require its own book. For now, a giant shout-out to everyone at the University of Wisconsin-Madison, Indiana University, the Fulbright program and the International Institute of Education, Boulder Media Women, the Community College of Denver, and the University of Colorado at Denver, among many other groups and organizations.

Generous thanks to the authors referenced throughout this book for lighting the path.

For mind, body, and soul, giant, kick-ass thanks to Arielle Schwartz and Juliet Seskind.

For incredibly loving (and adventurous) child care, thanks to Carissa Travis, Ashley Smith, and Samuel LaCasse, as well as all of my children's wonderful teachers.

Giant thanks to my fabulous friends, my fellow Ayreheads, and my wonderful community, including anyone who's ever answered one of my SOS's. I'm grateful for you all.

So much love to my fierce, funny, and rebellious mother.

Another sweet batch of love to my incredible children, who've taught me true joy and forgiveness, as well as healed me in ways I could never have imagined. I'm truly blessed to be their mother.

Finally, to my awesome, patient, kind, and funny husband Ken. I'm beyond blessed to have found such an incredible partner, and I can't imagine where I'd be without his unconditional love and support. Sure, he kicks my ass at times, but I wouldn't have it any other way.

About the Author

A former Fulbright Fellow, Tanja Pajevic received her M.F.A. from Indiana University, and has taught at the University of Colorado at Denver, the Community College of Denver, and Indiana University.

She is the recipient of numerous grants and awards, including a Hemingway Fellowship, a Kraft Fellowship, and a Developmental Faculty Award from the University of Colorado at Denver for her project "Writing as Healing." Tanja writes, blogs, consults, and teaches, as well as leads writing workshops around life's big transitions.

Her writing has been featured in various magazines, blogs, and websites, including *The New York Times*, Gawker, Scary Mommy, *Shenandoah*, and *Crab Orchard Review*, among others. Her personal blogs are Reboot This Marriage and The Rhythm of Grief.

Tanja lives in Boulder, CO, with her husband Ken and their two boys, Nico and Gabriel. She is currently working on a grief memoir.

Connect

Connect with Tanja in the following places:

Tanja Pajevic: http://www.TanjaPajevic.com

Reboot This Marriage: http://RebootThisMarriage.com

The Rhythm of Grief:
http://www.TheRhythmofGrief.com

Facebook: http://www.facebook.com/TanjaLPajevic

Reboot This Marriage Facebook page:
http://www.facebook.com/RebootThisMarriage

The Rhythm of Grief Facebook page:
http://www.facebook.com/RhythmofGrief

LinkedIn: http://www.linkedin.com/in/tpajevic

Twitter: @tpajevic (http://twitter.com/tpajevic)

NOTES

NOTES

NOTES

NOTES

NOTES

Made in the USA
Monee, IL
14 July 2022

99642507R10092